CHILDREN LIKE US
Toys and Games
AROUND THE WORLD

**Moira Butterfield
and Izzi Howell**

Cavendish
Square

New York

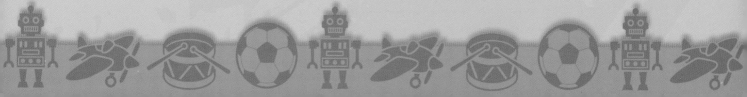

Published in 2016 by Cavendish Square Publishing, LLC
243 5th Avenue, Suite 136, New York, NY 10016

Copyright © 2016 Wayland / Cavendish Square Publishing, LLC

First Edition

Website: cavendishsq.com

This publication represents the opinions and views of the author based on his or her personal experience, knowledge, and research. The information in this book serves as a general guide only. The author and publisher have used their best efforts in preparing this book and disclaim liability rising directly or indirectly from the use and application of this book.

CPSIA Compliance Information: Batch #CW16CSQ

All websites were available and accurate when this book was sent to press. However, it is possible that contents or addresses may have changed since the publication of this book. No responsibility for any such changes can be accepted by either the author or the Publisher.

Cataloging-in-Publication Data

Butterfield, Moira.
Toys and games around the world / by Moira Butterfield and Izzi Howell.
p. cm. — (Children like us)
Includes index.
ISBN 978-1-5026-0852-9 (hardcover) ISBN 978-1-5026-0850-5 (paperback) ISBN 978-1-5026-0853-6 (ebook)
1. Toys — Juvenile literature. 2. Games — Juvenile literature. I. Butterfield, Moira, 1960-. II. Title.
GV1218.5 B88 2016
790.1'33—d23

Editor: Izzi Howell
Designer: Clare Nicholas
Proofreader: Izzi Howell
Picture researcher: Izzi Howell
Wayland editor: Annabel Stones

Picture credits:
The author and publisher would like to thank the following for allowing their pictures to be reproduced in this publication: Certe/Shutterstock.com, cover; p.3 (t-b) Martchan/Shutterstock, Christopher Futcher/iStock, rmnunes/iStock, Karen Struthers/Shutterstock, pp.4-5 (c) ekler/Shutterstock; p.4 (t) Christopher Futcher/iStock, (b) Pamela Moore/iStock; p.5 (tl) Vladislav Gajic/Shutterstock, (tr) Elena Yakusheva/Shutterstock, (b) Papa Bravo/Shutterstock; p.6 (t) Vladislav Gajic/Shutterstock, (bl) Berkut_34/iStock, (br) Alexander Chelmodeev/Shutterstock; p.7 ROB & SAS/Corbis; p.8 (t) Martchan/Shutterstock, (bl) Penny Tweedie/Corbis, (br) Gavran333/Shutterstock; p.9 fotoVoyager/iStock; p.10 (t) Christopher Futcher/iStock, (bl) Christopher Futcher/iStock, (br) jordache/Shutterstock; p.11 Don Mason/Corbis; p.12 (t) Aneese/Shutterstock, (b) rmnunes/iStock; p.13 Atlantide Phototravel/Corbis; p.14 (t) Papa Bravo/Shutterstock, (bl) whammer121736/iStock, (br) Karen Struthers/Shutterstock; p.15 Brian Mitchell/Corbis; p.16 (tl) migleon/iStock, (tr) Komsan Loonprom/Shutterstock, (b) Tyrone Turner/Assignment ID: 30032060A/National Geographic Creative/Corbis; p.17 Gavin Hellier/Robert Harding World Imagery/Corbis; p.18 (t) Pamela Moore/iStock, (b) Anatolii Babii/iStock; p.19 (t) arabianEye/Corbis, (b) Sandro Vannini/Corbis; p.20 (tl) bonga1965/Shutterstock, (tr) Elena Yakusheva/Shutterstock, (b) Guenter Guni/iStock; p.21 Lucian Coman/Shutterstock; p.22 (t) SEYLUL06/iStock, (bl) Dallas and John Heaton/Corbis, (br) David Ionut/Shutterstock; p.23 (t) zhykova/Shutterstock, (bl) jjspring/Shutterstock, (br) esolla/iStock; p.24 (t) Mike Kireev/Demotix/Corbis, (b) Richard Powers/Corbis; p.25 Mike Hutchings/Reuters/Corbis; p.26 (t) Christian Bertrand/Shutterstock, (bl) Martyn Goddard/Corbis, (br) pzAxe/Shutterstock; p.27 Denis Radovanovic/Shutterstock; p.28 (t) kickstand/iStock, (c) Blue Jean Images/Corbis, (b) Serbi/Shutterstock; p.29 (t) Paul Marcus/Shutterstock, (b) Mohammad Ismail/Reuters/Corbis; p.30 (l-r, t-b) Elena Yakusheva/Shutterstock, Anatolii Babii/iStock, Christopher Futcher/iStock, Lucian Coman/Shutterstock, David Ionut/Shutterstock, Guenter Guni/iStock, pzAxe/Shutterstock, kickstand/iStock, Alexander Chelmodeev/Shutterstock, SEYLUL06/iStock, rmnunes/iStock, Christian Bertrand/Shutterstock, migleon/iStock, Karen Struthers/Shutterstock; p.31 (l) Denis Radovanovic/Shutterstock, (r) whammer121736/iStock.

Design elements used throughout: Hein Nouwens/Shutterstock, ekler/Shutterstock, rassco/Shutterstock, lilac/Shutterstock, fongman/Shutterstock, lalan/Shutterstock, Dacian G/Shutterstock, microvector/Shutterstock, Wiktoria Pawlak/Shutterstock, vectorOK/Shutterstock, katarina_1/Shutterstock, zzveillust/Shutterstock, Alexey V Smirnov/Shutterstock, mart/Shutterstock, phil Holmes/Shutterstock, stockakia/Shutterstock, Divergenta/Shutterstock, Vector pro/Shutterstock, albund/Shutterstock, Karkas/Shutterstock, More Images/Shutterstock, Roblan/Shutterstock.

Printed in the United States of America

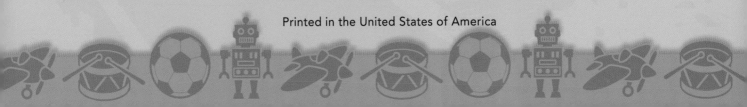

Contents

All Kinds of Toys and Games

What kinds of toys do children around the world play with? What games do they play? Are you ready to travel around the world and find out?

Learn about these Canadian snow tubes on page 10.

What do you think these American children are building? Find out on page 18.

Learn about this Polish girl's street game on page 6. Does it look like one you know?

Toys can be handmade. What is this Filipina girl weaving her toy from? Find out on page 20.

Find out about the Tanzanian board game called Bao on page 14.

Take a trip around the world to learn about the games and toys of children just like you!

City Games

Cities are crowded and busy. Children still find places to play. Even a sidewalk can become a playground if you have some chalk to draw with.

Hopscotch is a great game to play on pavement. You can draw a number grid and hop along it, like this Polish girl has done.

This hopscotch game is called escargot. That means "snail" in French. To play, you hop on one leg. You must jump over the dotted squares.

This streetball hoop can be moved to different places.

Ball games are a good way to play in small city spaces. These boys are playing streetball in the city of Volgograd, Russia. Streetball is a simple version of basketball.

Children around the world play clapping games. These American girls are singing a song called "Miss Mary Mack." They clap their hands together in a pattern as they sing.

Many different claps are done to the "Miss Mary Mack" song. In some, you clap your partner's hands. In others, you clap your own.

Country Playtime

In the country, there may not be a lot of parks or toy stores. Living far away from towns doesn't mean there's nothing to play with, though. These Ethiopian children are having fun with an old wheel.

An old wheel can become a toy to spin and chase.

These Aborigine children live in the Australian outback. They are playing with a boomerang carved from local wood. If they throw it the right way, it will fly back to them.

Boomerangs were made for hunting animals in the outback. They make great toys, too.

The curved shape of a boomerang helps it fly in a circle.

In Nepal, everyone in the village works together to build the ping swing.

In Ghorepani, Nepal, the children get a great new toy once a year. It is called a ping swing. The swing is made from bamboo poles and grass ropes. It's built as part of a yearly Hindu religious festival called Dashain.

Fun in the Snow

This Swedish boy is wearing gloves. They keep his hands warm while he plays in the snow.

There's only one rule in a snowball fight—if you are hit, you are out! However, most people stay in because snowball fights are so fun.

In the past, sleds were used to travel or move things. Today, they make a great toy. Traditionally, sleds were made of wood. This Norwegian girl is using a plastic sled with a handle.

This sled has a handle to help with steering.

These Canadian children are sledding downhill on snow tubes.

In the past, the blanket used in the blanket toss was made of sealskins. Now it is made from canvas and has handles.

Inuit communities in Alaska and Canada often play a traditional game called "blanket toss" at their spring festival. The blanket is used as a trampoline. The players pull it tight to make the person on it bounce.

Wonderful Water Toys

On a hot day, it's fun to cool down with water. In Florida, the city of West Palm Beach puts up a giant water slide every summer for children to play on.

This city water slide in Florida is nearly 0.25 mile (400 m) long!

This Thai boy is ready to soak his friends with his water gun.

At the Thai New Year's festival of Songkran, it's a tradition to pour water on other people. It is thought to wash away bad luck. Thai children often celebrate Songkran by shooting each other with water guns.

You don't need to get wet to have fun with water. These Tanzanian boys are getting ready to sail their toy boat on the ocean. Their handmade boat is made from recycled pieces of wood and plastic.

The extra pieces of wood on the sides of the boat help it float on the water.

Brilliant Board Games

The board game Bao is popular in East Africa. In Bao, you spread your pieces, called seeds, around the board. Then you make moves to take as many seeds from the other players as you can.

The seeds in Bao don't have to be seeds. They can be pebbles, shells, or even dung balls.

Some board games have been played for centuries. The Chinese game of Go is one of them. In Go, players have either black or white pieces. They move their pieces to try and cover the board with their color.

Chess may have first been played in India. It's such an old game that nobody knows for sure, though.

These Chinese children are playing Go.

This boy is using a Snakes and Ladders board made for people with little or no sight. He can feel each square and the patterns on the board.

This boy is using his fingers to play Snakes and Ladders.

Making Music

Chinese rattle drums have small wooden balls hanging from either side. They hit the drum when it is shaken. Maracas come from South America. They have seeds inside them that make a noise when the maracas are shaken.

Maracas always come in pairs, one for each hand.

The dragon on this Chinese rattle drum stands for good luck.

You don't always need a musical instrument to make music. This Brazilian boy is using an old plastic container as a drum.

This Brazilian boy is hitting a plastic drum with his hands to make a beat.

This Peruvian girl has her own set of South American pan pipes. Each little tube is made from a hollow reed of a different length.

Pan pipes are a common musical toy in South America.

Electronic Fun

The first robots were invented over 60 years ago. Today, you can buy remote-controlled robot toys, or even kits to build your own robot! Some schools around the world even have robot-building clubs.

Each child is putting together a different part of the robot toy.

With a cell phone or a tablet, you can download thousands of game apps to play with. Some apps teach you things. Other apps allow you to race cars or build your own town.

This tablet has a racing game. You move the car by touching the screen.

These girls from the United Arab Emirates have a unit to play games in their room.

These Egyptian boys share a unit in this desert tent.

Computer games are played all over the world. Some children have their own unit to play the games in their rooms. Other children must use a family unit to play. Here, two children play, and their friends wait for their turn.

Homemade Toys

This girl from the Philippines is making a toy from palm leaves. She is weaving the leaves together to make a shape. It's possible to make animals, dolls, hats, boxes, and more.

This girl is weaving a toy from palm leaves that come from the countryside around her home.

This fish is made from woven palm leaves.

This is a homemade Ethiopian TV toy. Inside the wooden frame is a tiny roll of paper. When the handle at the bottom is turned, the paper moves inside the toy. As it moves, it tells a story.

Ethiopian children can add their own drawings and stories to a TV toy.

This toy car has been made from recycled wire and tin cans. The Malawian boy made it from rubbish that would otherwise have been thrown away.

The boy uses a wire to pull his toy car.

All Sorts of Dolls

South American worry dolls are even given to children in hospitals to help them feel better.

These worry dolls are made for children in Guatemala and Mexico. Children tell their worries to the dolls before they go to bed. Then they pop the dolls under their pillows. The dolls take their troubles away during the night.

It can be hard to make doll-sized clothing. They are so small!

Dolls often wear national costumes. Lithuanian dolls wear traditional fabric belts and lace collars. Romanian dolls are often dressed in mini versions of the clothes that girls wear on holidays.

These Romanian dolls have wool hair that is braided in a traditional style.

Inside every Russian matryoshka doll is a set of smaller dolls! As you get further inside, the dolls get smaller and smaller. All the dolls are painted to look like they are wearing traditional Russian dresses and headscarves.

This girl is painting her own matryoshka dolls.

Traditionally, all the matryoshka dolls in a set are painted the same colors.

Super Sports

These Russian children are playing street hockey in a city square. The curved ends of their sticks make it easier to hit the ball. Hockey can also be played on ice. All the players wear ice skates.

Street hockey balls don't bounce. If they did, they might bounce away and get lost.

This boy swings his bat at the ball. If he misses, the ball may hit the wickets and he will be out.

All over India, you will see children playing cricket. These children are practicing on a field. It's traditional to wear white clothes when you are playing cricket.

Soccer is the world's most popular sport. Children play it in fields or streets around the world. Many of the world's greatest soccer players started out playing the sport with their friends.

This South African boy plays on a soccer club. They have a coach who teaches them how to play soccer.

All Sorts of Wheels

This Spanish boy is trying out some ramps on his scooter. He is at a park in Barcelona. To get moving, he needs to push one of his feet against the ground.

The first scooters were made from wooden boards and roller skate wheels. Today, scooters are metal.

Bicycles were first invented over two hundred years ago. Now children everywhere ride them. These Thai children have an unusual bike. It is a tandem bicycle for three!

This girl is learning how to ride a unicycle. It has only one wheel.

A tandem bicycle is fun for a family or a group of friends to try out.

This Canadian boy is in a skate park. Skateboarders can ride safely here.

The first skateboarders were Californian surfers in the 1950s. They wanted something to ride when there were no waves. In 1969, the first curved skateboard appeared. This made it possible to better control the board and do tricks.

Flying Toys

A paper airplane is one of the easiest toys to make. Most paper planes are made from a folded piece of paper. In some places, children make planes from palm leaves or wood.

This boy has a plane made from thin wood. They sell kits like this in toy stores.

This girl is getting ready to throw her paper plane.

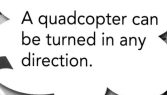

A quadcopter can be turned in any direction.

This tiny quadcopter has four rotating blades. They help it lift into the air and fly. The quadcopter has electronic controls that allow you to fly and steer it from the ground.

These Japanese kite fighters are using six-sided fighting kites.

Kite fighting is a popular sport in Afghanistan, Pakistan, and southeast Asia. The aim of kite fighting is to cut the string of someone else's kite in the sky. This boy is practicing with his kite near the city of Kabul, in Afghanistan.

This boy is flying a four-sided kite. This is a common kite for kite fighting in Afghanistan.

Art Station

Here are some ideas for getting creative and designing your own world!

- Design a toy car that could be made from recycled materials (look on page 21 for some ideas). Label the materials you would use.

- Design your own doll. It could be like one of the dolls on pages 22–23. What clothes would your doll wear?

- Design your own remote-controlled flying plane. It could even be a quadcopter like the one on page 28.

- Design a toy boat to float like the one on page 13. Think about where you would sail your boat—on the sea, on a park pond, in the bath?

Glossary

Aborigine A group of people who have lived in Australia for many centuries.

community A group of people who live together.

homemade Made by hand, not in a factory.

Inuit A group of people who live in the far north of North America.

national costume Clothes that are typical of a particular country.

outback A vast countryside region in the middle of Australia, where few people live.

palm A kind of tree that grows in areas where there is lots of warm weather.

recycled Used again in a different way.

remote-controlled Controlled by radio signal.

rotating Something that turns in a circular direction.

sense To feel something rather than see it.

streetball A simple version of basketball.

version An example of something.

Further Information

Websites

20 Toys and Games from Around the World
A closer look at the popular and unique toys and games.
multiculturalkidblogs.com/2014/12/08/20-toys-games-from-around-the-world/

Time for Kids – Around the World
This website offers a closer look at world cultures, including the toys and games unique to them.
www.timeforkids.com/around-the-world

Toys Around the World
A guide to toys from around the world.
www.windowsonwarwickshire.org.uk/spotlights/toysandgames/worldtoys.htm

Books

Dustman, Jeanne. *Cultures Around the World*. Huntington Beach, CA: Teacher Created Materials, 2014.

Galimberti, Gabriele. *Toy Stories: Photos of Children from Around the World and their Favorite Things*. New York, NY: Abrams, 2014.

Peterson, Casey Null. *Games Around the World*. Huntington Beach, CA: Teacher Created Materials, 2011.

Index